THE LAST REMAINING SEATS

To John —
Have the courage to dream and the persistence to make it a reality.

THE LAST REMAINING SEATS:

Movie Palaces of Tinseltown

Photographs by
Robert Berger and Anne Conser
with an introduction by Stephen M. Silverman

HENNESSEY+INGALLS

Santa Monica 2004

First published by Balcony Press, Los Angeles, 1996.

Reprinted with permission by

Hennessey + Ingalls
214 Wilshire boulevard
Santa Monica CA 90401

www.hennesseyingalls.com

ISBN 0-940512-41-6 (paper)

Architecture + Film, No. 5.

Library of Congress Cataloguing-in-Publication Data
Berger, Robert, 1959-
    The last remaining seats : movie palaces of Tinseltown / photographs by
Robert Berger and Anne Conser ; with [text and] an introduction by Stephen M.
Silverman.
        p. cm. -- (Architecture + film ; no. 5)
    Originally published: Los Angeles, Calif. : Balcony Press, 1997.
    Includes bibliographical references.
    ISBN 0-940512-41-6
    1. Motion picture theaters—California—Los Angeles--Pictorial works. 2. Los
Angeles (Calif.)--Buildings, structures, etc.—Pictorial works. I. Conser, Anne. II.
Silverman, Stephen M. III. Title. IV. Series: Architecture and film ; 5.
    NA6846.U62L673 2004
    725'.823'0979494--dc22
                            2004054101

1

INTRODUCTION

The night Robert Berger attended a Jazz on Film program in the fall of 1990, he encountered the unexpected. Descended from two generations of Angelenos, Berger was only vaguely familiar with his hometown's civic center, which was not too unusual given California's post-World War II demographics. The neglected urban outpost was perhaps

Corner of 5th and Broadway, ca. 1932

known to Baby Boomers only as the once pristine backdrop for such vintage '50s television programs as *Dragnet* and *Superman*, neither acclaimed for authenticity (the latter, in fact, passed off the stately 1928 Los Angeles City Hall as the headquarters of the Daily Planet).

What immediately compelled Berger, a Santa-Monica-based architectural photographer, was not the uncharacteristic (for Southern California) density of downtown structures, or even the flea markets with Spanish signs hawking everything from fried *platanos* to phony Chanels, but the singularly ornate venue of the evening itself, the Orpheum Theater. "How could such an incredible example of entertainment history be left to crumble in a town where movies are the biggest industry?" he wondered. With brass doors, marble floors, gold-leafed ceiling, crystal and bronze chandeliers (augmented by bold torchères and intimate cove lighting), and costly Scalamandre-silk-embroidered French trimmings garnished by bare-breasted bronze women — who looked like willing kidnap victims from the Paris Opera House — the opulent Orpheum, built in 1926, once ranked among the grandest theatrical halls in the world.

Its still-palatial interior also claimed the patron-friendly innovation of a lobby-to-mezzanine automatic elevator and, below the stairs, an even greater rarity: an air-conditioned lounge. Trimmed in rich oak, with a fireplace large enough to cook in, the subterranean setting looked not so much like the practical public room it was built to be (it serves as the gateway to the men's room) as it did an English gentleman's club. Crowning the Orpheum's splendors was a thirteen-rank, three-manual Wurlitzer organ, with metal and wooden pipes capable of simulating the orchestral sounds of no fewer than 14,000 pieces. "You just don't see architectural details like these in Los Angeles," noted Berger.

The next morning he related his discovery to Anne Conser, his business partner since 1985 and a friend since their days as photography students. For Conser, Berger's tale of the Orpheum rang an otherworldly bell. She had just been told by a psychic that "during a past life in the 1800s, I had been a vaudeville performer who was killed after a performance while trying to break up a brawl between my husband and an overly enthusiastic fan." Confronted with Berger's discovery of a vaudeville theater, Conser wondered whether to tune him in or run like the devil — until remembering that, according to the same psychic, "My next life as a nun didn't work out well, either."

According to Conser "Robert has a very scientific approach to how we shoot our jobs, whereas I will try anything so long as I arrive at the right solution." Their professional relationship has been described as yin and yang, prompting Berger to note diplomatically, "It's a good thing that our photographs are not accompanied by an audio tape of our debates during the sessions." Both concurred, however, that it was Berger who pushed Conser into a second and more thorough inspection of the Orpheum, despite downtown's seedy reputation.

Any uneasiness they may have felt was superseded by Berger's determination. The photographers' plan of action: "We found the director of the theater, showed him our portfolio, and persuaded him to let us photograph the Orpheum." The 2,190-seat Orpheum opened on February 15, 1926, based on an architectural design by the Pascal-trained, Beaux-Arts-inspired, San Francisco-based G. Albert Lansburgh (1876-1969), whose major commission was that city's Opera House. From 1909 to 1930, in addition to designing Orpheum theaters for Kansas City, St. Louis, and New Orleans, as well as the Martin Beck in New York, Lansburgh was one of the most important performing-arts hall designers in Los Angeles. In 1926 alone he created three memorable, diverse interiors: the 6,700-seat, Moorish Revival Shrine Civic Auditorium; the grandiose (with its deep boxes and opera stage) 1,036-seat El Capitan Theater; and the Orpheum.

The $1.9-million, French-Renaissance style theater was the fourth building in Los Angeles to operate under the revered Orpheum banner, which was started in the mid-1880s by San Francisco theater owner Gustav Walter. Food and drink were served, and variety acts performed

Loew's State Theater, 1932

(they would eventually be termed "vaudeville"). Under new ownership, in 1898 the Orpheum "circuit" was born and several theaters across the country were leased to house its impressive acts, including one particular stand-up comedy team of growing renown:

Gracie Allen: "I have brains, you know."
George Burns: "Oh, you do?"
Gracie Allen: "I have brains I haven't even used yet."

So key was the addition of a new Orpheum to Los Angeles that Lansburgh's ornate 1926 structure usurped the preeminent position for top bookings from the nearby 1,250-seat Palace (also designed by Lansburgh, and also at first named the Orpheum), until then, the Southern California stage home to the Marx Brothers, Sarah Bernhardt, Will Rogers, and the powerhouse entertainer who helped launch the talkies, Al Jolson. Onto the boards of the new Orpheum stepped Sophie Tucker, Bill "Bojangles" Robinson, Ted ("Is everybody happy?") Lewis, and a comedian with superb delivery named Jack Benny. When he played the Orpheum, the joke went, Benny used to dash across the street between shows to charm a certain lingerie seller — who later became his wife — Mary Livingstone.

Salesgirl One: "Look, it's Jack Benny!"
Salesgirl Two: "Jack Benny!"
Salesgirl Three: "Why, it's Jack Benny!"
Mary Livingstone: "Who's Jack Benny?"

If the Bennys' rendezvous alone didn't earn the Orpheum a standing in popular history, then consider a singing act called the Gumm Sisters. After their debut at the nearby Loew's State, they played the Orpheum, where sitting in the crowd was an MGM talent scout. On September 27, 1935, the studio signed the most promising member of the trio, thirteen-year-old Frances. She became Judy Garland.

When vaudeville collapsed and the coming of talkies changed movies forever, more modern and thematic movie palaces drew crowds west into the formerly theater-deprived oases of Hollywood and Beverly Hills. The Orpheum adjusted. In December of 1929, management substituted the Orpheum's long-standing two-a-day vaudeville bookings for movies, reopening with RKO's *Hit the Deck*. Unfortunately, the title proved apropos: attendance hit the deck. To arouse it, the Orpheum instituted Star Nights, where on many a Monday patrons could see, for instance, cowboy star Tom Mix in the house. Mix always took two seats, one for himself, the other for his ten-gallon hat.

The Depression closed the Orpheum in 1932, though the theater reopened the following September with a bill of ten vaudeville acts and a movie double feature with newsreel and cartoon, all for the cut-rate admission of a quarter. The scheme was the brainchild of a young impresario, Sherill Corwin. Under his care, the Orpheum prospered for a dozen years, reaching its zenith in the 1940s with exclusive entertainment bookings which included Cab Calloway and Duke Ellington. Lena Horne set the all-time box-office record at the Orpheum: $55,000 of ticket sales in one week in 1944, the same year she sang "Love" in MGM's "Ziegfeld Follies."

The headliners on the show were Jimmie Lunceford and his band, recalled the ever-stunning singer. But then "some of the guys in the band," she said, let word slip that she was replacing the great Black singer June Richmond, whom the Orpheum had originally hired, "because, at the moment, because of the picture, I was hotter." Horne felt crushed. "I was hurt for June's sake, too," she said. "I don't think she ever believed, through all the years afterward, that I had not connived to take the booking away from her. The morning I opened, she was there in the first row, watching me silently."

When vaudeville at the Orpheum finally died in the mid-'50s, the theater began to present young singers — Aretha Franklin, Sam Cooke, the Everly Brothers — as accompaniments to film features, until a '60s influx of Spanish-speaking patrons put an end to live programming. Hollywood movies were shown subtitled in Spanish. By then, too, suburbia was stretching out and movies in general were losing their adult audience. As producers began to woo teen tastes, young moviegoers themselves didn't seem to mind being cooped up in newly hatched neighborhood multiplexes.

Such changes in Los Angeles combined to leave the once vibrant Orpheum stage vacant, until movie makers rediscovered the playhouse at the end of the '60s. Scenes for

United Artist's Theater

William Wyler's 1968 *Funny Girl* were shot there, notably Barbra Streisand's Act II "Swan Lake" parody. Production continued, though infrequently, for three more decades on the site — witnessed by glimpses of the Orpheum in Oliver Stone's *The Doors*, Tim Burton's *Ed Wood*, *The Last Action Hero* with Arnold Schwarzenegger, a small-screen version of *Gypsy* starring Bette Midler, and television episodes of *Murder, She Wrote* and *Seinfeld*.

The theater's history is a casebook study of the uncertain fortunes of an entertainment palace. As the millennium approaches, its future as a movie house is uncertain. A perfect parallel is New York's Radio City Music Hall, built in 1932 to showcase movies and to pre-feature stage acts, but since the 1980s an exclusive and profitable venue for concerts and live events. In an effort to promote the Orpheum's use as a setting for live entertainment, volunteer preservationist groups argued for letting

the Orpheum serve as the permanent home to the city's Philharmonic Orchestra in need of a new concert hall. "With downtown movie attendance virtually nil, what we'd like to promote is an adaptive re-use of places like this," said Conser, standing not far from the Orpheum's brass box office as crowds of Saturday shoppers passed without even a glance at the marquee.

Once the Orpheum was documented, Berger and Conser wanted to expand their theater portfolio. "Our intention was to photograph as many of these palaces as we could, and bring images of them to the public, because the public was no longer coming to them. What they didn't know when they started was that they were about to embark upon an archeological expedition into the movie palaces of Tinsel Town, an arduous journey that would demand six years of their lives.

By the 1930s, they learned, the seven-block Broadway radius between Third Street and Olympic Boulevard flaunted fifteen picture palaces, among the largest American collection outside of New York. What was unique to Los Angeles, they also discovered, was that so many of the structures, though non-operational, were at least still standing, and in their own way able to speak volumes about the region's past.

Culture met commerce in Los Angeles' Broadway at the turn of the century. Hamburger's Department Store, built in 1907, was once the largest such emporium west of Chicago and the forerunner of later downtown stores such as Robinson's, the May Company, and The Broadway. With double-decker public transport hustling shoppers through the heavily trafficked neighborhood, store-window displays appeared in second-floor picture windows, just as, inside the 1911 Palace Theater, the Ladies' Lounge was one story above ground, outfitted with a similar vantage point for its anxious patrons awaiting their gentlemen escorts.

When it came to making movies, the pioneers preferred to live and work downtown rather than in the more conservative Hollywood. Among the earliest of these was Francis Boggs, from the (Colonel William) Selig Polyscope Company of Chicago. In 1907, Boggs shot along the coast, in La Jolla. Moving north, he assembled a temporary studio on a rooftop at the corner of Los Angeles' Eighth and Olive Streets; a year later, also on Olive, he built what is believed to be L.A.'s first permanent studio — in a former Chinese laundry. No joke: in 1909, the first dramatic feature filmed entirely in California, *The Heart of the Racing Tout*, was produced there. Other visionaries followed, including D.W. Griffith, who started wintering in Los Angeles in 1910.

When it came to providing showplaces, downtown Los Angeles' ground-breaker was real-estate developer William H. "Billy" Clune, who built theaters and produced his own pictures to exhibit in them. Clune had been an investor in Griffith's 1915 *The Birth of A Nation* and later owned what is now Raleigh Studios. In 1910, Clune opened his 775-seat Cameo, designed on the outside as a free-standing Renaissance Revival structure of cast iron, with an interior of marble, plaster, leaded glass, and a galaxy of electric lights. Admission to this wonder world: one nickel. Also known as Clune's Broadway, the Cameo was the fourth theater in Los Angeles to be built exclusively for movie exhibition, making it, until its 1991 conversion into commercial space, the longest-operating movie theater in the state — if not the country.

Though not a "palace," the Cameo holds the distinction of having opened three years before New York City's Regent Theater, which is generally considered the first movie palace in the United States. The Regent's architect, Thomas Lamb, responsible for some three hundred cinemas, chiefly designed for MGM magnate Marcus Loew. Lamb preached that "to make our audience receptive and interested, we must cut them off from the rest of city life and take them into a rich and self-contained auditorium." In comparison, by 1913 Los Angeles' theater community was already part of the city's fabric.

On September 26, 1910, Los Angeles welcomed the 1,400-seat Pantages, built to resemble a Beaux Arts English music hall. This may explain the boisterous opening-night headliner: New York sensation Sophie Tucker, "the last of the red-hot mamas." Not that Alexander Pantages himself wasn't a nonconformist: having launched his career producing variety shows during the 1890s Klondike Gold Rush, he worked his way south. One secret of his success — also a reason for his downfall — was his policy of hiring only female ushers. One allegedly framed him for statutory rape, working as a shill for Boston business-man and political patriarch Joseph P. Kennedy, who, in the late '20s, en-gineered a hostile takeover of the Pantages chain. At stake was Kennedy's need to control theaters for the movies of his then mistress, Gloria Swanson. Faced with expensive legal bills, the already ailing Pantages was forced to sell the namesake business that he had built sin-gle-handedly. Once convicted, Pantages served some of his fifty-year sentence, only to be acquitted two years later. He died in 1936. In the end, Kennedy took over the Pantages chain, once the largest privately owned vaudeville circuit in the world. A lasting relationship it was not — quickly tiring of the movie business, and more tellingly of Swanson, Kennedy sold out, leaving the Pantages chain in the hands of the Warner brothers, who quickly dropped live acts in favor of movies.

In 1920, ten years after Pantages built his first, eponymous, theater downtown, he opened another, leaving the original to be referred to as the Broadway Pantages. In 1925, the Broadway Pantages became the Arcade, named for the colossal Arcade office building next door. By then stripped of its elegance and its side boxes plastered over, what was once a downtown showplace was sadly frayed. The Arcade's rescue and symbolic re-launch into a new era arrived in 1938, in the form of an ex-tensive makeover by architect S. Charles Lee, (1899-1990), the most prominent and prolific force behind tastes and trends in California cin-ema design.

Born in Chicago, where Frank Lloyd Wright wielded his influence, Lee emigrated west in the 1920s, where from his Hollywood office he designed nearly four hundred theaters during the '30s and '40s, most of them in California. Lee's guiding motto: "The show starts on the sidewalk."

According to his biographer, Maggie Valentine: "The physical environment of the theater began, literally, at the sidewalk, where a colorful terrazzo pattern set it apart from the usually dirty concrete sidewalks of the surrounding commercial district; overhead, a marquee formed a canopy." This way, she stated, Lee had succeeded in symbolically setting the theater "apart from all other adventures of the city. Cinema was an industry that sold an experience and a memory, not a product."

Lee's role, driven by the potent designs of the Art Deco period, was to reinforce a patron's memory of time spent in the dark. His first Los Angeles assignment was the Tower, an exercise in opulent compactness and innovation, with tiny baroque splendors that included tile, stained glass, sculpted ceilings, and a new technical item: sound. In 1927, *The Jazz Singer*, starring Al Jolson, held its West Coast premiere here. At the Arcade, Lee streamlined the outer lobby, masking its artistic murals and dome with black tile and terrazzo . In the '60s, as at the Orpheum, the Arcade shifted to a diet of Spanish-language and heavy action films. By the late 1980s, overseas developers had bought the house, along with the adjacent Cameo and the 1,600-seat, Art Deco gem, the Roxie. In 1992, the Arcade's projectors were stilled and its lobby sliced up into several small stores.

The Tower Theater, 1928

At the "newer" Pantages, at Seventh and Hill, the only movie-related vestiges to remain, other than the awesome gilded lobby ceiling and interior overhead mural, were trademark Warner Brothers shields decorating the cavernous skeleton. By the early '70s the theater had become the International Church of Compassion. Finally, the seats were ripped out to be replaced by jewelry counters. Since the early 1980s, Alexander Pantages's 1920 flagship has been a retail mart.

What had begun, simply enough, as a matter of curiosity for the photographers, somehow became a labor of politics: some landlords, it developed, objected to trespassers on their premises, even ones carrying the harmless artillery of cameras and lighting equipment. "They were suspicious of our motives," said Berger. "Some didn't like the idea that we might profit from these photographs." "Others," added Conser, "were concerned that by documenting the interiors we would expose how much of these historic properties had been damaged or destroyed."

Not that this discouraged their sense of adventure. "So there we'd be," said Conser, referring to having to shoot after business hours in those sites that did offer access, "staying up way past our bedtimes, and going bump in the dark with a small legion of quirky theater buffs and other, less benign, beady-eyed nocturnal creatures." "Rats," clarified Berger. "The most exciting moment for us is always entering a theater for the first time," continued Conser. "It's like walking into an ancient Egyptian tomb." Some have been sealed for what seems just as long.

Perhaps their greatest find was what had once been the most lavish palace of all, the Los Angeles Theater. This Versailles in miniature, containing 2,200 seats, veered from designer S. Charles Lee's usual Deco leanings. "This building and his Tower Theater must be viewed as belonging to his 'Motion-Picture Baroque' period," observed architect Patrick McGrew, who has made a study of Southern California's landmarks. "The

The Chinese Theater, 1930

Los Angeles Theater's rich and flamboyant French Renaissance eclecticism, which was a copy of San Francisco's legendary 'lost' Fox Theater, concealed some fancy planning that allowed for retail shops to be integrated into the facade...Street space on Broadway at this period was simply too valuable to be taken up by the bulk generated by an auditorium."

Yet what an auditorium it was — and for the most part remains although the Los Angeles has been shuttered since 1994. Some experts consider it, though atypical of Lee, his crowning achievement. As determined by the National Trust for Historic Preservation: "None of his more than four hundred theaters could match the opulence of the Los Angeles, or the cost — $1.2 million. Lee added thirty new draftsmen to his staff to keep pace with the five-month construction schedule." Independent film exhibitor H. L. Gumbiner hired Lee and instructed him to ignore the Depression and to deliver a world-class house able to compete with New York's Broadway theaters. To assist, Lee hired architect S. Tilden Norton, later an associate architect on the Wilshire Boulevard Temple (1922-29). His father, Isaac Norton, had owned the estate on which the Los Angeles was built.

What Lee and Norton delivered was a controlled environment worthy of Walt Disney. As described by the Los Angeles Conservancy:

The Los Angeles...boasted a number of unusual amenities, including an electric indicator to monitor available seats and blue

neon floor lights to guide patrons through the aisles. Mothers with crying babies could retire to either of two soundproof Crying Rooms above the loge, while older children romped in a staffed playroom in the basement. Patrons seeking refreshment might visit the theater restaurant or smoke in a designated room with built-in cigarette lighters. Ladies would congregate in a glamorous restroom featuring sixteen private compartments, each finished in a different marble, or mix with the men in the walnut-paneled lounge, where a periscope-like system of prisms relayed the feature film from the auditorium to a secondary screen.

The historic première attraction on January 30, 1931 (only eight days after completion of post-production) was Charles Chaplin's pantomime masterpiece, *City Lights*, with Charlie himself in attendance, along with his guests, Professor and Mrs. Albert Einstein. Also on hand was the aristocracy of Hollywood: the King Vidors, the Cecil B. DeMilles, the Darryl F. Zanucks, the Joseph Schencks, the John Barrymores, the Jack Warners, Hedda Hopper, Marion Davies, and the ubiquitous Gloria Swanson. "The main street was packed with people for several blocks," Chaplin recalled. "Police cars and ambulances were attempting to plow through the crowds." In spite of this overt example of public enthusiasm, to such an extent that the cops threatened tear gas on the unmanageable mass, Chaplin admitted, "How I loathe first nights."

"The most incredible thing happened," said Chaplin of a moment during the third reel. "Suddenly, in the middle of the laughter the picture was turned off! The house lights went up and a voice over a loudspeaker announced: 'Before continuing further with this wonderful comedy, we would like to take five minutes of your time and point out to you the merits of this beautiful new theater.'" Chaplin's reaction: "Where's that stupid son of a bitch? I'll kill him!" With it all, Chaplin's movie was a success, as was Gumbiner's theater, artistically speaking. Financially, it was not. It was said that after filing for bankruptcy a year after the Los Angeles opened, Gumbiner stopped to point out the merits of the suits he was selling at his new place of employment — Brooks Brothers.

"An imp," said Myrna Loy, taking delight in her realization that "he looked a little like Harpo." The figure remembered during a late 1980s interview was the West Coast showman, Sid Grauman (1879-1950). Though he was born in Indianapolis and got his first dose of show business, like Pantages, by putting on shows for isolated Yukon miners, Grauman was a California phenomenon. He convinced his father, an ex-vaudeville minstrel, to stake him in the new motion-picture industry, and together they opened San Francisco's Unique Theater, a giant, 800-seat (kitchen chairs, actually) nickelodeon on Market Street that went up in the fiery aftermath of the 1906 earthquake. By 1915, Sid and David were a force, owning several theaters in northern California and one in New York, but the ambitious son convinced his father to dispose of the properties so that he could embark upon his grandest undertaking to date, the accurately named Million Dollar Theater.

Albert C. Martin (exterior) and William Lee Woollett (interior) designed what is acknowledged as the first palace in Los Angeles officially created to show movies. If New York had its Cathedral of the Motion Picture in its Roxy, which didn't open until 1927 — then Los Angeles, the country, in fact, had this earlier prototype courtesy of Grauman. The Million Dollar's exuberant façade brings legendary figures from the arts together with nature's icons from Western Americana (longhorn skulls for instance) in a variation of Spanish Rococo known as Churrigueresque. On-stage, however, was pure Grauman. Taking a cue from his fanciful façade, he blended the theme from his movie into the theme of his stage acts. Make no mistake, either, as to whose theater this was. When the 2,345-seat Million Dollar opened on February 1, 1918, with the William S. Hart Western, *The Silent Man,* the slogan appearing above the title was "Sid Grauman Presents."

Once the Million Dollar was successfully launched in 1919, Grauman assumed management of the two-year-old, 870-seat Rialto (Woollett, again, redesigned the interior). The Rialto contained a more modest program policy of musical acts and features, though one typical 1919 "Grauman Prologue" included "Barcarole" performed by the theater's orchestra, followed by a costume pageant of gowns worn in the main attraction — nothing less than Gloria Swanson in Cecil B. DeMille's social statement, *Male and Female.*

Next for Grauman was his first theater in Hollywood, the 1,800-seat Egyptian (Meyer & Holler, designers), which had the good fortune to open just before Tut fever swept the country. The *al fresco* forecourt leading to the Theban temple's auditorium was "overseen" by stately plaster heads of the pharaohs, while twin black Dogs of Annubis statues inside the lobby seemed to welcome delighted patrons.

On October 18, 1922, the theater opened with Douglas Fairbanks's *Robin Hood,* though just as much attention was paid Grauman's costumed, bearded Bedouin — complete with spear — who greeted each guest (and remained during the two-a-day, reserved seat run of every picture). *Singin' in the Rain* premièred there, as did earlier hits ranging from Chaplin's *The Gold Rush,* Fairbanks's *Thief of Baghdad,* and Mary Pickford's *Sparrows,* right through the decades to *My Fair Lady.* Among its final "hard-ticket" attractions was *Funny Girl.*

"The Chinese was more festive in its day," actress Joan Bennett remembered in the early 1980s, "but the Egyptian was more prestigious." Grauman's most famous creation — also his most lasting, despite the unsportsmanlike removal of his name by a new owner in the 1970s — was his 1927 Chinese, diagonally across the street from the flashy El Capitan. The overgrown, jade-colored pagoda has been described as the biggest star in Hollywood, the movie capital's "town hall, mother church, forum, Prado, and hall of fame." So synonymous with glamour was the Chinese that the ultimate Hollywood movie about Hollywood movies, 1951's *Singin' in the Rain,* opens its story with a Chinese première. "We didn't shoot the scene there," confessed the film's co-director, Stanley Donen, in 1996. "MGM bought ten feet, at five dollars a

TOWER THEATER

Built on the site of an earlier, 650-seat house, the 900-seat Tower capitalized upon its powerful Baroque elements and prominent, if narrow, corner location to allow its precocious 27-year-old architect S. Charles Lee his personal homage to "Movieland Mannerist." As noted by architect Patrick McGrew, Lee "utilized windows that evoke the Paris Opera, columns from LeDoux, Moorish details, Spanish arches, and miscellaneous Italian elements — all executed in gleaming terra-cotta — to complete one of the most compelling buildings on Broadway." The opening night feature, October 12, 1927, was the hugely forgettable *The Gingham Girl.* Within a month, however, Warner Brothers delivered something momentous: the West Coast premiere of *The Jazz Singer.* Equipping this first theater in Los Angeles for historic Vitaphone, Lee told the *Times:* "I had tremendous problems because I didn't know how big the sound horns would be." The talkies stayed, but the Tower has been long shuttered. The indignities began in 1971, when damage after an earthquake forced the lowering of the theater's crowning namesake, though the interior is still used privately as a film and video location.

*In addition to being Los Angeles' inaugural "talkie" house, S. Charles Lee's
opulent baroque fantasy was the first to be "mechanically refrigerated."
The Tower dazzled on many a score.*

29

STATE THEATER

Beginning with a string of peep shows around Manhattan and Cincinnati, exhibitor Marcus Loew (1870-1927) owned 400 cinemas coast to coast by 1912. Eight years later, he was supplying himself with his own product by purchasing Metro Pictures, which in 1924 merged with Samuel Goldwyn and Louis B. Mayer's companies to become MGM, wholly controlled by Loew. As was the case with the company flagship in Times Square, the Los Angeles counterpart was named Loew's State. As the largest brick-clad building in Los Angeles, the 2,450-seat State — designed by Mark Hopkins Hotel architects Charles Weeks and William Day — enjoyed a three-decade run that began on November 12, 1921. Its all-star bills consisted of live acts with movies (for an admission less than the average vaudeville ticket), connected into "theme" shows staged by the brother-sister dance team of Fanchon and Marco — whose chorines included Janet Gaynor and Myrna Loy. In 1928, the Meglan Kiddie Review delivered six-year-old Frances Gumm to the State footlights. Later, as Judy Garland, she lasted at MGM until 1951, which was just as long as the State survived as the studio's first-class downtown house. Thereafter, Garland staged memorable comebacks. The State, alas, never has.

As a picture palace, the State remained the most successful theater
on Broadway for more than half a century. Offering MGM
movies was its not-so-secret weapon.

34

PALACE THEATER

Believed to have been modeled after the Casino de Municipale in Venice, with its decorative exterior of laughing faces on brackets and gremlins astride window arcades, this 1911, 2,200-seat Orpheum house presented W. C. Fields, Sarah Bernhardt, Will Rogers, and some of the greatest animal acts in vaudeville. Harry Houdini stirred the greatest sensation, stationing an ambulance curbside in case any of his stage magic caused an audience member to faint. Permanent elements include four exterior panels depicting the muses of Song, Dance, Music, and Drama (sculpted by Domingo Mora, a Spaniard whose work also decorated New York's old Metropolitan Opera House), as well as a rare interior artifact for the generally tolerant Los Angeles: a second balcony that until the 1930s was designated "Negroes only."

With money purportedly no object, the Los Angeles went up
in only five months. Once built, the theater was so staff-intensive,
remembers one former patron, there were attendants whose sole
job it was to insure that smokers' cigarettes remained lit.

54

MILLION DOLLAR THEATER

Originally called Grauman's, this 2,345-seat, 1918 Spanish palace was the work of the architectural firm founded in 1906 by Albert Carey Martin, whose other commissions included St. Vincent de Paul Church, Los Angeles City Hall, the May Company on Wilshire and Fairfax, and the Department of Water and Power headquarters opposite the Music Center. Working from the fairy tale "The King of the Golden River," impresario Sid Grauman wove fantasy decoration into the Million Dollar — rechristened in honor of its price tag, though rumored to have actually cost twice what the name claimed. By the '20s he turned the operation over to Paramount Publix, which, until the company went bankrupt in the early '30s, kept the property as a first-run house (Valentino's *Son of the Sheik* played here in 1926, the same year the star died). Vaudeville and movies filled the bill through World War II, whereupon Metropolitan Theaters assumed ownership in 1945 and booked names such as Billie Holiday and Cab Calloway. From the 1950s through '80s, Mexican movies and stage shows took over, until the Million Dollar's reincarnation as a church in 1992. Recently, the upper floors of the theater building have been converted into housing units.

As late as the 1970s, the Million Dollar featured live stage shows accompanying the movie feature. Another unique feature was located on the second floor: a liquor bar, one of the few in an L.A. cinema.

BELASCO THEATER

New York at the turn of the century had David Belasco, "the biggest theatrical manager of that time," said Dorothy Gish. Los Angeles had family member Edward Belasco, whose elaborate four-story, Spanish-Moorish Revival confection — designed by Morgan, Walls & Clements — opened November 11, 1926. Edward's gift was in enticing New York talent like Tallulah Bankhead and Helen Hayes to play for him whenever they came West to make movies. The hallmarks of Edward's house included excellent acoustics, an expansive "green room," and a ballroom on the mezzanine that could hold as many as four hundred. "Although the ground-level façade has been remodeled," said a Los Angeles Conservancy representative, "conquistadors in 'pineapple' surrounds remain in place above the second story." Having at one time been the home of the Metropolitan Community Church, the Belasco is currently privately owned and available for rental as a movie or video location.

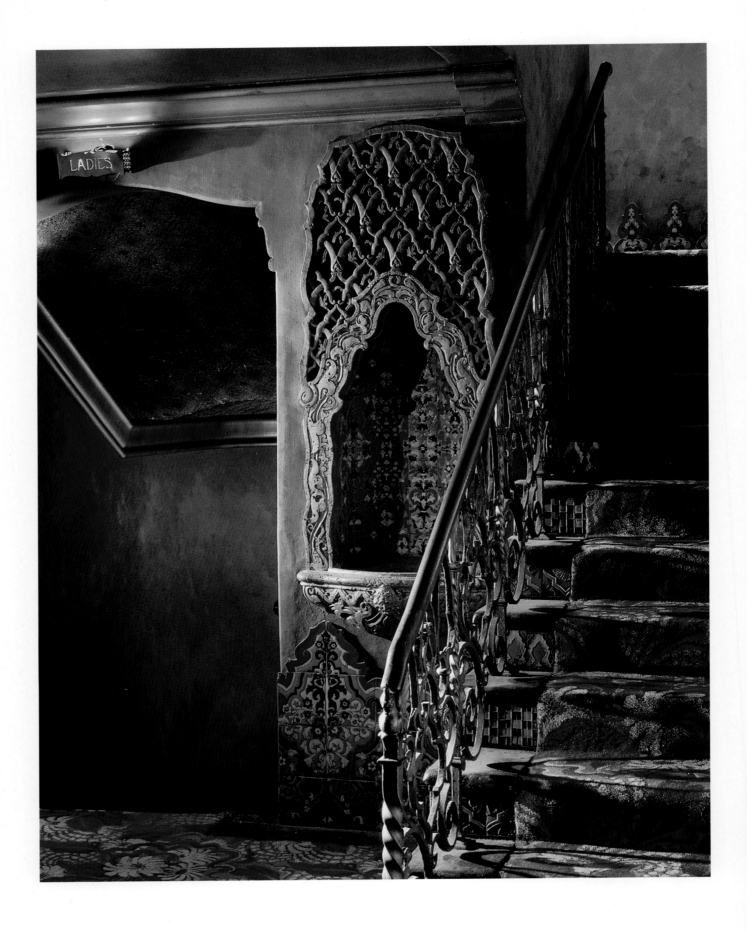

64

CHINESE THEATER

Meyer & Holler designed it, and the Egyptian and El Capitan's developer C. E. Toberman — not Sid Grauman, who tended to lease his theaters — actually built this iconographic temple to the motion picture, albeit per Grauman's fanciful specifications. Since 1927, nearly 170 stars have literally left their marks on the place (note forecourt), and the string of releases to play here — *King of Kings, King Kong, The King and I, Some Like It Hot, West Side Story, Mary Poppins, Star Wars, Batman,* to name a few — serve as testament to the Chinese's drawing power beyond that of simply a tourist magnet. Since the last reserved-seat engagement, *Hello, Dolly!,* in 1969, Grauman's Chinese hasn't been quite itself. The place was renamed Mann's Chinese in 1972, and seven years later, two lackluster modern "companion" screens sprouted up on the property.

*The Chinese, the showplace that has hosted more premieres than
any other Hollywood theater began construction on Armistice
Day, 1925. Its first rivet was driven by Anna May Wong.*

EL CAPITAN THEATER

A preservationist's dream, this 1,500 seat house was born again at the age of 65 after a total renovation by the Walt Disney Company in 1991. Opening May 3, 1926 with the London smash "Charlot's Revue of 1926" (starring Gertrude Lawrence, whose movie biography *Star!* coincidentally played the theater 51 years later), the El Cap features a Morgan, Walls & Clement Period Revival exterior with East Indian detailing, and a G. Albert Lansburgh South-Seas-motif interior. The structure's adjacent footage and upper floors were long occupied by the Barker Brothers Furniture Company, Southern California's largest. As for the theater's programming, when no movie exhibitor would risk the wrath of William Randolph Hearst, Orson Welles personally opened *Citizen Kane* here on May 9, 1941. The next year, Paramount took over and changed the house name to match the studio's. Well into the '60s, despite the magnificent architectural underpinnings having been camouflaged by drab draperies, the Paramount presented such distinguished first-runs as *Sunset Boulevard, War and Peace, Vertigo, Gigi, The Music Man,* as well as a curious string of medical movies: *Doctor Zhivago, Dr. Dolittle,* even *Doctor's Wives.* The theater's reopening in 1991 featured a festive première of *The Rocketeer.*

During a 1942 première here, the curbside floodlight at the El Capitan had to be amber, in observance of World War II's black-out rules. Anything stronger might have signaled enemy aircraft.

EGYPTIAN THEATER

Mother Time and Mother Nature were not kind to Sid Grauman's 1922 Tut-like Meyer & Holler wonder. The forecourt that Audrey Hepburn floated down for the 1964 première of *My Fair Lady* was chained up in 1992, and, thanks to mildew, earthquake damage, and vandals, Hollywood's first authentic movie palace became a product of sad neglect. Still, evidence revealed that some of the kooky hieroglyphic murals as well as the sunburst above the panoramic screen and the jungle forecourt could be saved. Early in 1996 it was announced that the non-profit American Cinematheque was taking over the Egyptian with plans for a total "rehabilitation." Said Len Betz, project manager for the City of Los Angeles Community Redevelopment Agency: "This is the darling of Hollywood." Perhaps Mothers Nature and Time are not be so bad, after all.

Sid Grauman instituted the "Hollywood première" at the Egyptian: klieg lights, crowds in bleachers, stars entering on a red carpet. Debbie Reynolds stomped her way through the still-presentable forecourt in 1964, for The Unsinkable Molly Brown.

HOLLYWOOD PACIFIC THEATER

Warner Brothers built this $1.25-million, 1928 Renaissance Revival (with a touch of Movie Palace Rococo) theater, office, and retail complex. "Tame in comparison to its exotic Hollywood neighbors," huffed one architectural journal. G. Albert Lansburgh designed its opulent Moorish interior, including an awesome semi-circular lobby. The first feature, when the house was still called the Warner Brothers Theater: Conrad Neagle and Dolores Costello in *Glorious Betsy.* In the late '40s, Carol Burnett worked as a Warners usher. In the early '50s, *This is Cinerama* played here-and, slightly improved, the gloriously impractical camera process was still going strong in 1968, when Stanley Kubrick's *2001: A Space Odyssey* drew starry-eyed young crowds to partake of Kubrick's mastery on screen and, by then, Lansburgh's anachronistic splendors around it. "Triplexed" in subsequent years, Hollywood's once-largest theater is today a disappointing shadow of its former self.

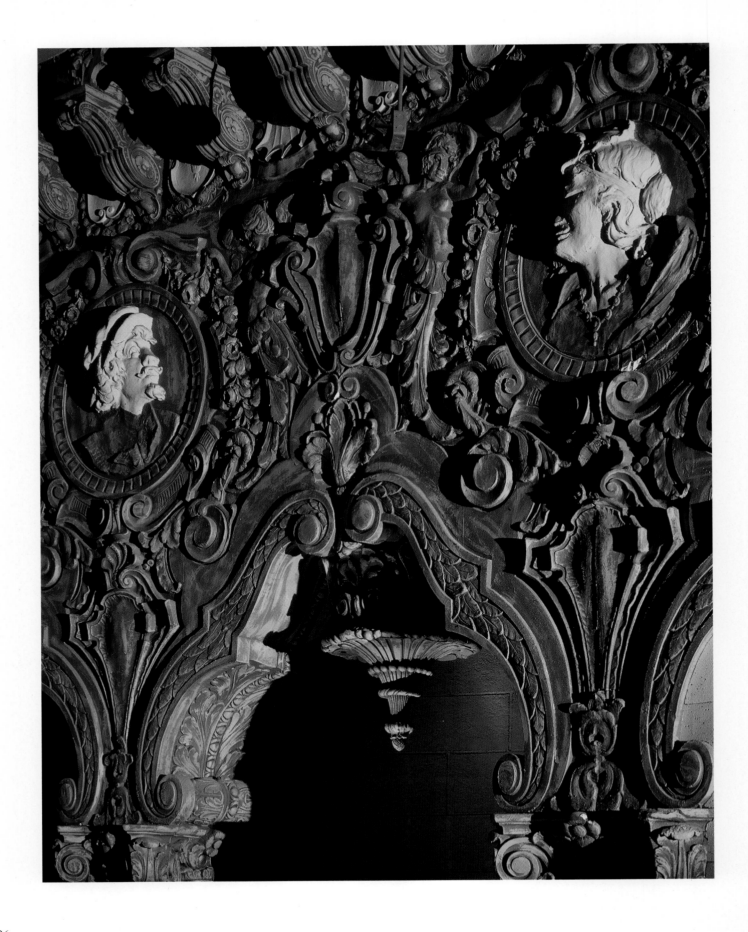

Developer Wayne Ratkovich proved the Wiltern's knight in shining armor. In the mid-'80s he saved the Wilshire Boulevard Art Deco temple from the wrecker's ball.

RIALTO THEATER

Among the least known of California's major theater architects was L.A. — for Los Angeles — Smith, who died at the height of his career in 1926, a year after this Moorish temple to vaudeville and movies opened (with Universal's *What Happened to Jones?* and a Fanchon and Marco stage specialty). Smith's other commissions included East Los Angeles' Brooklyn Theater, Highland Park's Highland, and the Arabian-style Beverly Theater in Beverly Hills, lone since converted to retail space. Said one appreciation of the Rialto: "Note the Batchelder tile drinking fountain in the lobby complete with picture tiles. The auditorium features plaster ornament, colorful stenciling, organ screens supported by harpies (half woman, half vulture), and a glaring mythological beast with red eyes staring down from the proscenium arch." Such an evil gaze may have motivated Robert Altman to use the alleyway behind the Rialto to stage the murder in *The Player.*

Depression-era bonuses for patrons of the Rialto included a free
pass to the on-premises miniature golf course, a chance to take
home cash during Bank Night and, on the inevitable Dish Night,
a china plate to add to the domestic dinner table.

WARNER GRAND THEATER

Considered an Art Deco extravaganza on a neighborhood scale, the Warner Bros. Theater, as it was called when it opened on January 20, 1931, was the first theater in the South Bay to be equipped with sound (by 1930, the area already had its noble share of picture palaces: the Fox Cabrillo, the Strand, the Barton Hill, the Globe). Ground was broken on the Warner on June 18, 1930, with little Jack Warner Jr. lifting the first shovel. His father referred to the theater itself as "The Castle of Your Dreams," and opening night Barbara Stanwyck and Joan Blondell were on hand to laugh at Joe E. Brown in *Goin' Wild*. As were theater designers B. Marcus Priteca and Anthony B. Heinsbergen. Today the Grand is a newly restored component of San Pedro's civic center.

Despite the Depression, the '30s brought suburban expansion to once-rural Southern California. In San Pedro, movie mogul Jack Warner built his studio's Grand — which it was, literally.

AVALON THEATER

Muralist John Gabriel Beckman, whose commissions included Grauman's Chinese, rode a glass-bottomed boat around Catalina Island's Sugarloaf Point for inspiration before decorating the nine panels encircling the Avalon Theater's inner loggia. Originally intending to do something Greek, Beckman instead leaned toward a *sui generis* Aquarium Deco, with a smattering of Botticelli, whose "Birth of Venus" he duplicated over the proscenium. When this sumptuous, 1,250-seat (before two front rows were extracted for being too close to the screen) house opened in 1929, it served as an integral component of island owner (and chewing gum magnate) William Wrigley's streamlined Spanish Colonial casino and ballroom structure (Webber and Spaulding, architects). So acoustically fine was the theater—and still is, given its only changes have been the additions of a 1949 refreshment stand and a 1953 Cinemascope screen—that the engineers of Radio City Music Hall studied it in 1931. During World War II the Avalon became a classroom for seamen and a USO center presenting Bob Hope, Kate Smith, and Spike Jones. By the '50s, the Miss Catalina Pageant was a regular attraction, though movies still bring in the crowds, every evening in summer and most nights the remainder of the year.

When they shot on and around Catalina Island, Hollywood heavies C. B. De Mille, Louis B. Mayer, John Ford, and Erich von Stroheim used the Avalon to view their daily rushes. In 1946, a legit play premiered here: The Gentle Approach, starring relative newcomer Robert Mitchum.

SELECTED BIBLIOGRAPHY

Alleman, Richard. *The Movie Lover's Guide to Hollywood*. New York: Harper & Row, 1985.

Birdsong, Toni Page. *Sound of Silents,* Los Angeles Downtown News, August 19, 1996.

Chaplin, Charles. *My Autobiography*. New York: Simon and Schuster, 1964.

Chung, Roy. *Egyptian's Dynasty to Be Reborn,* Westside Weekly (Los Angeles). February 18, 1996.

Glines, Carole. *A Last Hurray for Hollywood,* Historic Traveler (Harrisburg, Pennsylvania), May/June 1995.

Hall, Ben M. *The Best Remaining Seats*. New York: Bramhall House, 1961.

Horne, Lena, and Schickel, Richard. *Lena*. New York: Doubleday & Co., 1965.

Kobal, John. *People Will Talk*. New York: Alfred A. Knopf, 1985.

Margolies, John, and Gwathmey, *Emily. Ticket to Paradise*. Boston: Little, Brown, 1991.

May, Linda L. *Save the Theaters!,* Industrial Photography (Melville, New York), September 1994.

McGrew, Patrick, and Julian, Robert. *Landmarks of Los Angeles*. New York: Harry N. Abrams, 1994.

Naylor, David. *American Picture Palaces*. New York: Prentice Hall Press, 1981.

Naylor, David. *Great American Movie Theaters*. Washington, D.C.: The Preservation Press, 1987.

Robinson, David. *Chaplin*. London: Collins, 1985.

Simmons, Steve. *Admission to the Past,* View Camera (Sacramento), January/February 1995.

Valentine, Maggie. *The Show Starts on the Sidewalk*. New Haven: Yale University Press, 1994.

Webb, Michael (editor). *Hollywood: Legend and Reality*. Boston: Little, Brown, 1986.

Willman, Chris. *Kings of the Big Screen,* Los Angeles Times, Calendar, June 16, 1996.

DOWNTOWN

Orpheum, 1926	842 S. Broadway	Architect: G. Albert Lansburgh
Tower, 1927	802 S. Broadway	Architect: S. Charles Lee
Globe, 1913	744 S. Broadway	Architect: Morgan, Walls & Morgan
State, 1921	703 S. Broadway	Architect: Weeks & Day
Los Angeles, 1931	640 S. Broadway	Architect: S. Charles Lee and S. Tilden Norton
Palace, 1911	615 S. Broadway	Architect: G. Albert Lansburgh
Arcade, 1910	534 S. Broadway	Architect: Morgan & Walls
Roxie, 1932	518 S. Broadway	Architect: J.M. Cooper
Million Dollar, 1918	307 S. Broadway	Architect: Albert C. Martin and William Lee Woollett
Belasco, 1926	1060 S. Hill St.	Architect: Morgan, Walls & Clements
Mayan, 1927	1040 S. Hill St.	Architect: Morgan, Walls & Clements
Pantages, 1919	7th and Hill St.	Architect: B. Marcus Priteca

HOLLYWOOD

Chinese, 1927	6925 Hollywood Blvd.	Architect: Meyer & Holler
El Capitan, 1926	6838 Hollywood Blvd.	Architect: G. Albert Lansburgh and Morgan, Walls & Clements
Egyptian, 1922	6708 Hollywood Blvd.	Architect: Meyer & Holler
Hollywood Pacific, 1927	6433 Hollywood Blvd.	Architect: G. Albert Lansburgh
Wiltern, 1931	3790 Wilshire Blvd.	Architect: G. Albert Lansburgh

OUTLYING AREAS

Rialto, 1925	1023 Fair Oaks, Pasadena	Architect: L.A. Smith
Warner Grand, 1931	478 W. 6th St., San Pedro	Architect: B. Marcus Priteca
Avalon, 1929	Catalina Island	Architect: Weber & Spaulding

A NOTE FROM THE PHOTOGRAPHERS

Due to the reluctance of a few theater owners to having their properties photographed, you may notice a conspicuous absence of a notable theater or two from what we originally hoped would be a comprehensive documentation of the remaining movie palaces of Los Angeles. Though unable to realize that goal completely, we hope that you will share our sense of wonder and awe of the treasures that still exist amongst the high rises and strip shopping malls, if you only know where to look.

ARCADE THEATER

Originally named the Pantages, this 1,400-seat house was the first theater in Los Angeles to be leased by the Orpheum circuit's chief competitor, Alexander Pantages. Though he never could match his rival in prestige, Pantages still had flair; opening night, September 26, 1910, he had his programs printed on silk. The headliner for the occasion was Barnold's Dog & Monkey Pantomime in "A Hot Time in Dogville," featuring Dan, a four-legged canine drunk. Dan was followed by a newcomer, Sophie Tucker. "According to newspaper accounts of the opening," reads one history of the Pantages (renamed the Arcade in 1925, after the new office building next door), "the paint was barely dry and the stage manager was lauded for bringing the show off without a hitch." One 1919 headliner was a string bean of a comic named Stan Laurel, who, in another seven years, would be teamed with the rotund Oliver Hardy, for the movies and for the ages.

GLOBE THEATER

In January of 1913, West Coast impresario Oliver Morosco gambled by opening his 1,303-seat Beaux Arts Globe not as a vaudeville house or nickelodeon, but as an elegant dramatic playhouse whose niceties included rows of seats accommodating patrons who weighed more than 200 pounds. What Morosco did not include: intermission music, which he deemed an intrusion. Instead, he filled the Globe's orchestra pit with brilliant foliage, leaving patrons to converse without having to shout over loud instruments. After producing the wildly successful Abie's Irish Rose, Morosco departed in the '20s, and the Globe, renamed the President, went to the Henry Duffy Players (who included Edward Everett Horton). During the Depression, movie newsreels took over, continuing throughout World War II. Afterward, the Globe reclaimed its original name, though its fortunes faded simultaneously with downtown's. In 1958, a Mexican Wax Museum opened in the basement, to abet the Spanish-language programming upstairs. In 1987, concrete leveled the floor from the lobby to the stage, so a permanent indoor swap meet could supplant what had once been the first serious playhouse in Los Angeles, fat-man section and all.

PANTAGES

Alexander Pantages presided over his empire from within the towering Beaux-Arts-style Pantages Downtown Building. The 1919 structure, with Pantages' courtly, 2,000-seat theater as its cornerstone, was the second home of Pantages vaudeville in Los Angeles, designed by the prolific, Seattle-based architect B. Marcus Priteca (who also designed the art-deco Hollywood Pantages in 1929, spectacular but not accessible to the photographers.) The Pantages, as this Hill Street house was called, had its share of shame, too. In 1923, an argument broke out between two related performers, resulting in the fire-eater fatally shooting his cousin, then turning the gun on himself. Such color is a thing of the past, however: since the early '70s, what was once a stage-show and movie Valhalla — and the Warner Bros. downtown flagship for sound motion pictures — has been a cut-rate Tiffany's theater.

ROXIE THEATER

No relation to the Cathedral of the Motion Picture in New York — which was the Roxy (1927) — this 1,600-seat jewel opened November 25, 1931, and eschewed old world elegance for new-fangled Zigzag Moderne. "Characteristics," proclaimed a 1992 Los Angeles Conservancy appreciation, "include the stepped roofline of the theater's exterior elevation, angular grillwork and chevron ornament on the facade, and a spectacular terrazzo sunburst in the sidewalk." Designed by architect and builder John M. Cooper, the Roxie was also the last downtown picture palace to be constructed before first-run movies settled into Hollywood. Since the late 1980s, what appears to have been the perfect backdrop for an Astaire-Rogers musical has served instead as the setting for a swap meet.

LIST OF PHOTOGRAPHS

ACKNOWLEDGMENTS

Stephen M. Silverman would like to acknowledge Margaret Denk, Peggy Glance, Martha Kaplan, Carol Morgan, Stephen Paley, Doris Tourmarkine, and Alice K. Turner. The photographers would like to thank Ellen Harrington at the Academy of Motion Picture Arts and Sciences, Jon Olivan and Ed Kelsey of Friends of The Orpheum, Ken Steuck of Orange Coast College, Francie Kugelman of The Gallery At 777, and Arnold Schwarznegger. Special thanks to the Los Angeles Conservancy for the use of our book title "The Last Remaining Seats," the name of their annual classic film series held in downtown L.A.'s historic theater district and for keeping the love of these old theaters alive through their walking tours.

The following archival images were provided courtesy of Security Pacific National Bank Collection/Los Angeles Public Library:

Million Dollar Theater, circa 1946

Premiere of "Morocco," 1930, at the Chinese Theater
    Corner of 5th and Broadway, circa 1932

Tower Theater, 1928

United Artist's Theater

Loew's State Theater, 1932, is provided courtesy of B'Hend & Kaufman Archives/Terry Hegelsen Collection

THE PHOTOGRAPHERS

Alan Shaffer

Robert Berger and Anne Conser have been working together since 1983, when they were both students in the photography department at Orange Coast College in Costa Mesa, California. Photographing architecture and interior design for their clients has taken them around the world, and their work has appeared in numerous books and periodicals. Their shared fascination with historic properties has led to this personal project that has consumed much of their time for the past six years. Limited edition prints of the photographs in this book are available from Berger/Conser Photography, Santa Monica, California.

THE AUTHOR

Stephen M. Silverman's five previous books include *David Lean* and *Dancing on the Ceiling: Stanley Donen and His Movies.* Born and raised in Los Angeles, he currently is the Editor of PEOPLE Daily Online, for the New Media division of Time-Warner Inc., and he teaches at the Columbia University Graduate School of Journalism in New York.